The Joy of Piano Duets

For centuries duet playing has held and continues to hold
a fascinating attraction for the student, the teacher,
the professional musician. One of the most pleasurable aspects
of music-making, it always provides an enjoyable experience
to both player and audience. In addition, it has definite
pedagogical benefits.

The Joy Of Piano Duets contains colorful examples of music
from the classics to folk songs and jazz. The arrangements
are equally easy for both players with the melody alternating
between the two.

Robert Schumann advised pianists, "Don't omit any opportunity
to play with others." It is sound advice. We trust that this
collection will be a source of pleasure to "one piano-four hands"
enthusiasts the world over.

Exclusive Distributors:
Hal Leonard
7777 West Bluemound Road
Milwaukee, WI 53213
Email: info@halleonard.com

Hal Leonard Europe Limited
42 Wigmore Street
Marylebone, London, W1U 2RY
Email: info@halleonardeurope.com

Hal Leonard Australia Pty. Ltd.
4 Lentara Court
Cheltenham, Victoria, 3192 Australia
Email: info@halleonard.com.au

Printed in the EU

Contents

Bourrée
from Violin Sonata No. 2

Secondo

Johann Sebastian Bach

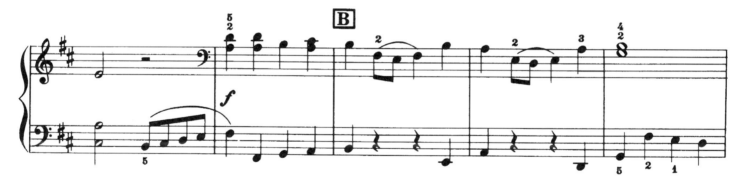

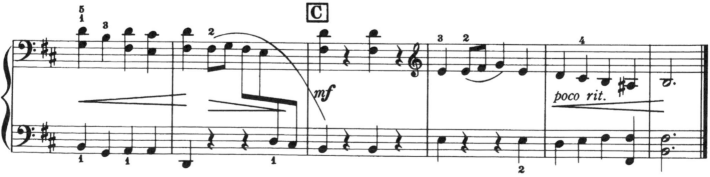

Bourrée
from Violin Sonata No. 2

Primo

Johann Sebastian Bach

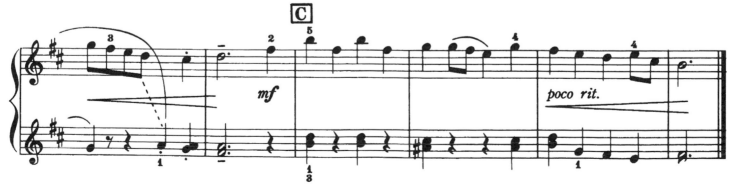

The Trout

Franz Schubert

Moderately   **Secondo**

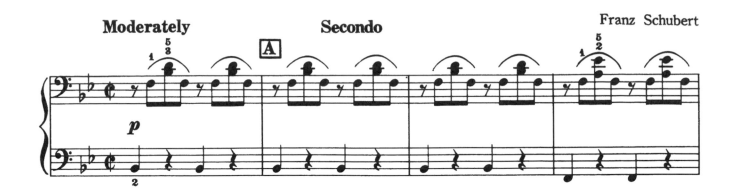

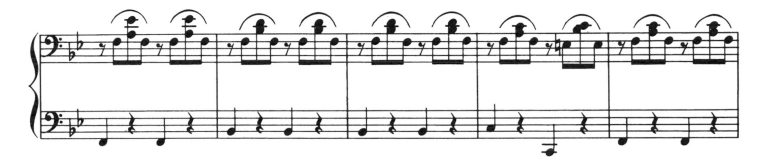

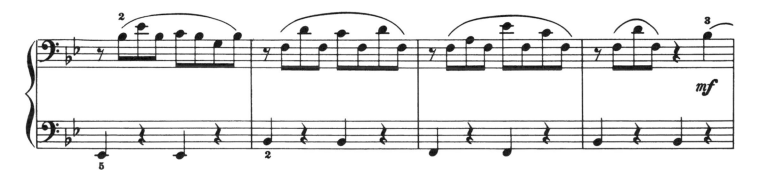

The Trout

Primo

Franz Schubert

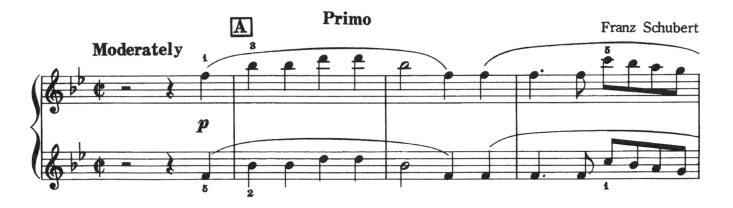

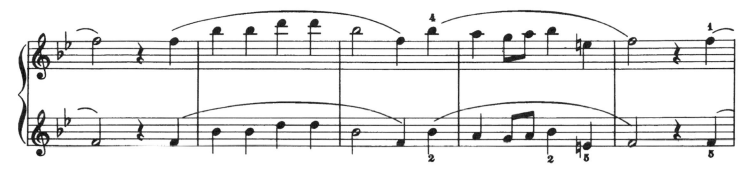

"The Metronome"
Theme from Symphony No. 8

Secondo

Ludwig van Beethoven

Lively, mechanical motion

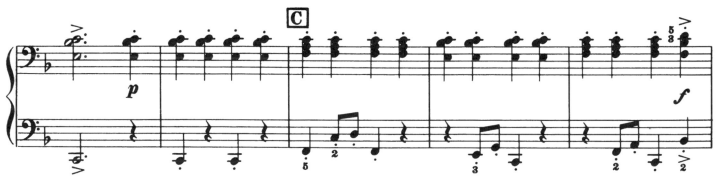

"The Metronome"
Theme from Symphony No. 8

Primo

Lively, mechanical motion

Ludwig van Beethoven

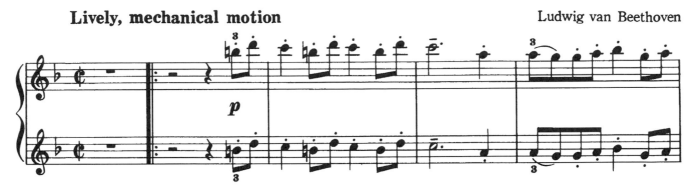

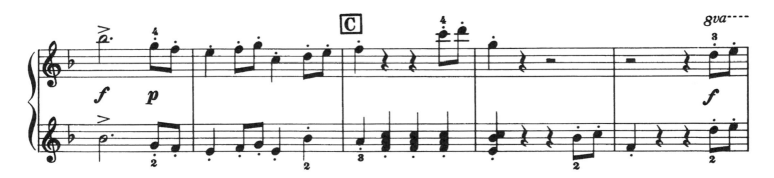

Arioso

Secondo

Johann Sebastian Bach

Moderately slow

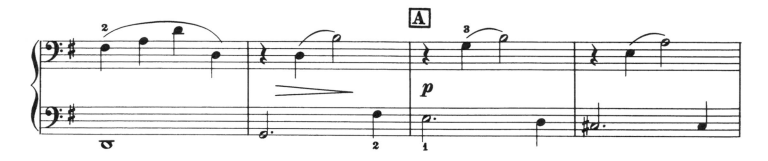

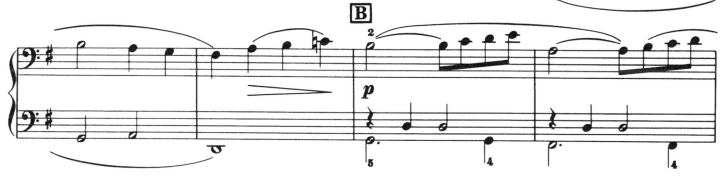

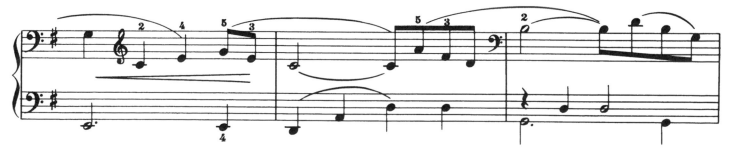

Arioso

Primo

Johann Sebastian Bach

Rondino
Theme from Cello Concerto in D

Secondo

Joseph Haydn

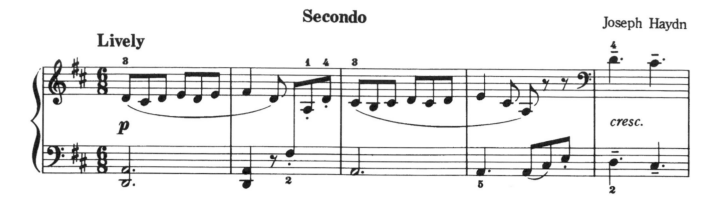

D.C. al Fine

Rondino
Theme from Cello Concerto in D

Primo

Joseph Haydn

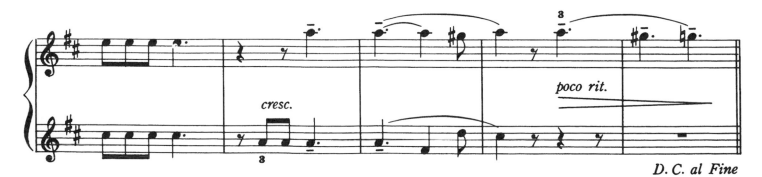

D.C. al Fine

Caprice No. 24

Secondo

Niccolo Paganini

Caprice No. 24

Niccolo Paganini

Duet from "Don Giovanni"
("La ci darem la mano")

Wolfgang A. Mozart

Secondo

Duet from "Don Giovanni"
("La ci darem la mano")

Wolfgang A. Mozart

Melody in Waltz Time

Theme from String Quartet No. 2

Secondo

Alexander Borodin

Moderately; with a lilt

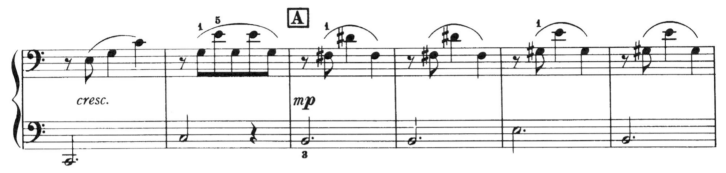

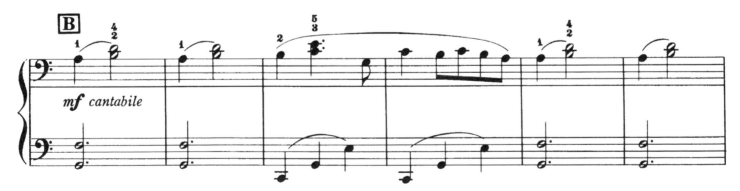

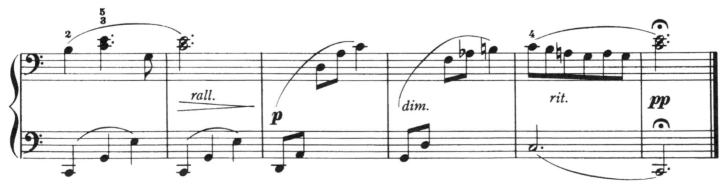

Melody in Waltz Time

Theme from String Quartet No. 2

Primo

Alexander Borodin

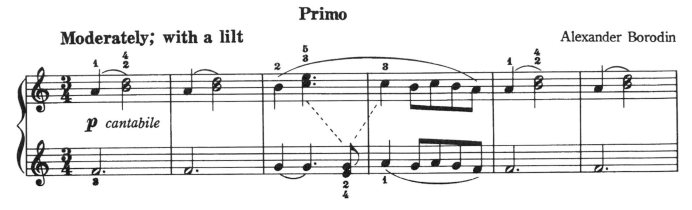

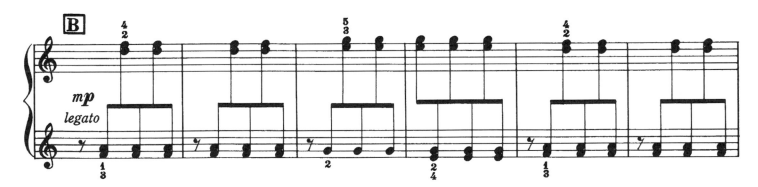

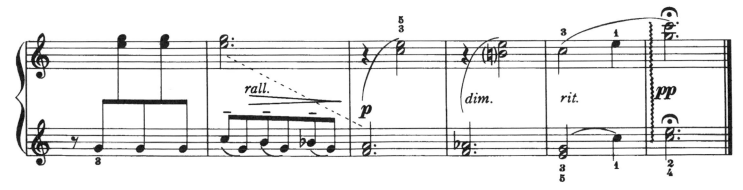

Gavotte from "Classical Symphony"

Secondo

Serge Prokofieff

Gavotte from "Classical Symphony"

Primo

Serge Prokofieff

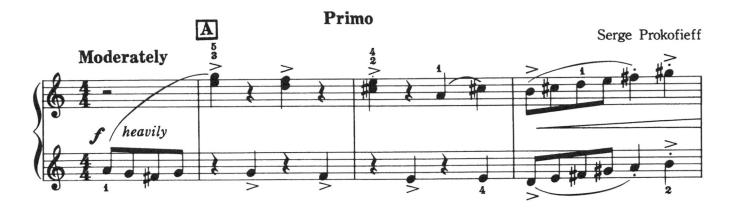

The Musical Snuffbox

Secondo

Lively, mechanical motion

Anatol Liadov

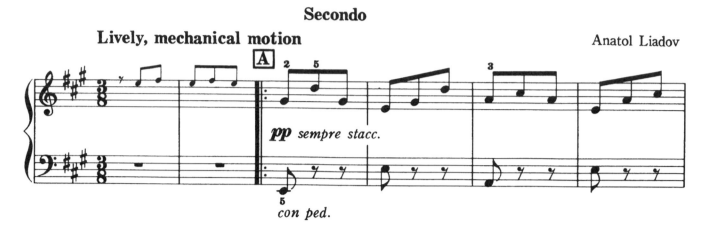

The Musical Snuffbox

Primo

Anatol Liadov

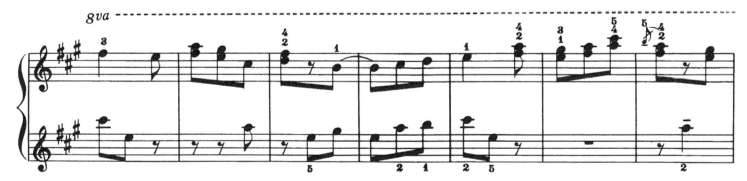

Secondo

The Harmonious Blacksmith
(Theme)

Moderately **Secondo**

Georg F. Händel

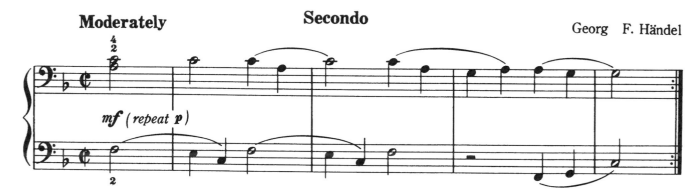

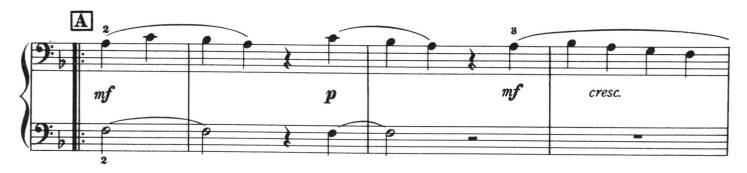

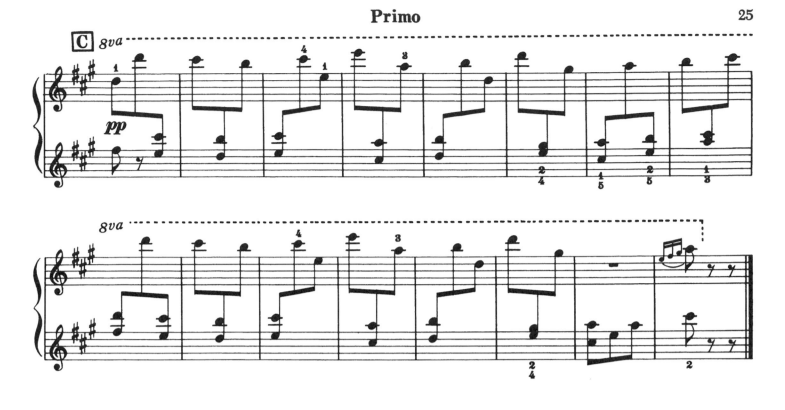

The Harmonious Blacksmith
(Theme)

Primo

Georg F. Händel

Frolic

Secondo

Béla Bartók

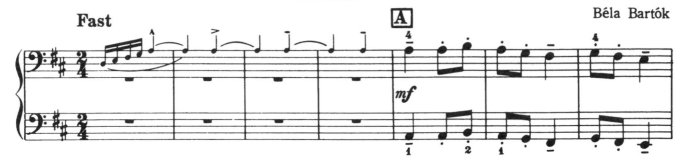

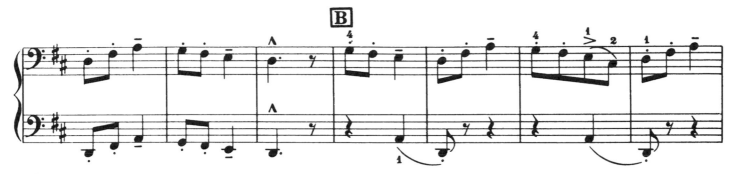

Frolic

Primo

Béla Bartók

Lullaby from "The Firebird"

Secondo

Igor Stravinsky

Lullaby from "The Firebird"

Primo

Igor Stravinsky

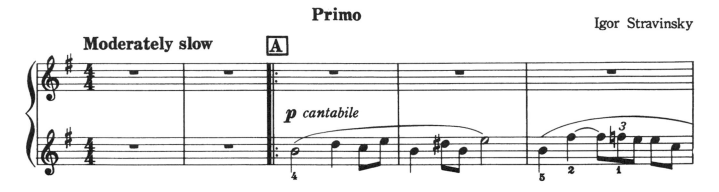

Trepak

Russian Dance from " The Nutcracker"

Secondo

Peter I. Tchaikovsky

Very lively

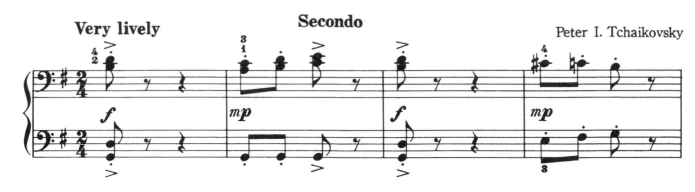

Trepak
Russian Dance from "The Nutcracker"

Very lively　　　　　　　　Primo

Peter I. Tchaikovsky

Minuet
from "A Little Night Music"

Secondo

Wolfgang A. Mozart

Gaily moving

Minuet
from "A Little Night Music"

Primo

Wolfgang A. Mozart

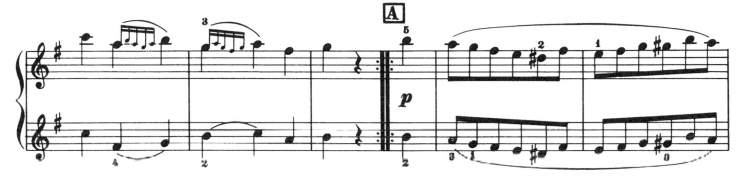
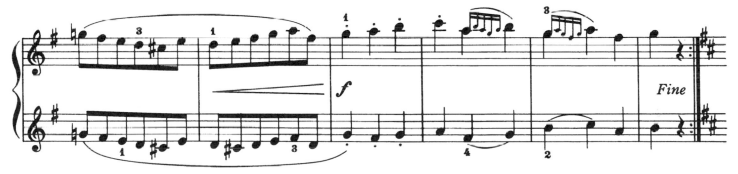

Secondo

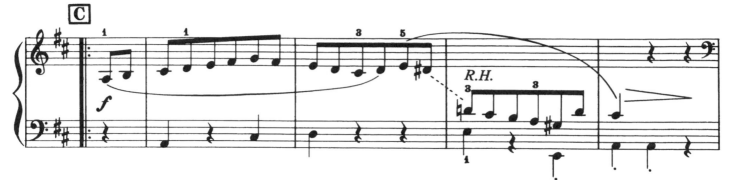

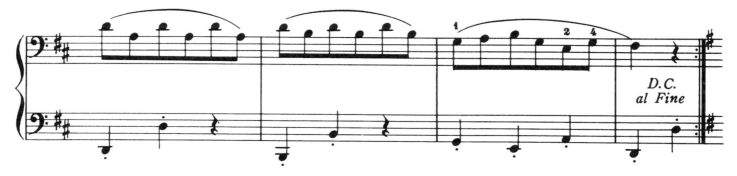

The Streets of Laredo

Secondo

Cowboy Song

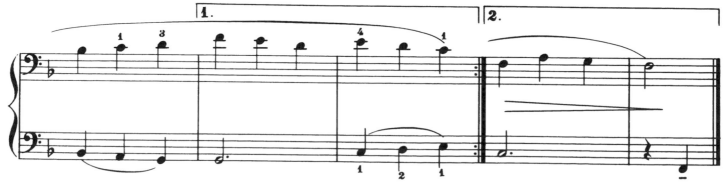

The Streets of Laredo

Primo

Cowboy Song

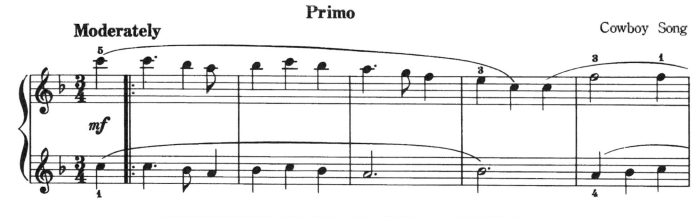

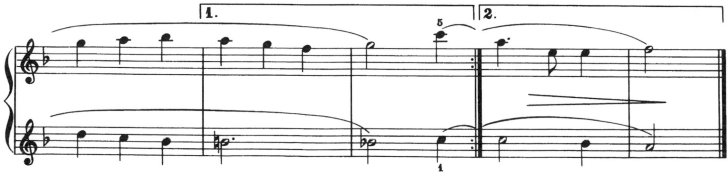

The Comedians' Galop

Secondo

Dmitri Kabalevsky

The Comedians' Galop

Primo

Dmitri Kabalevsky

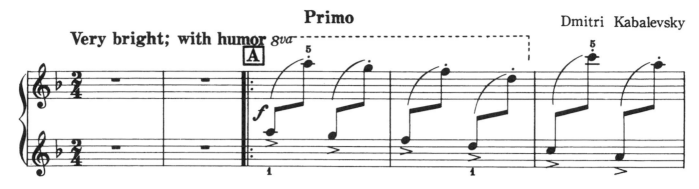

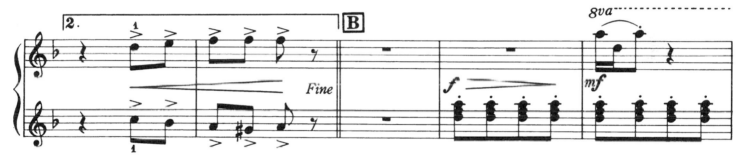

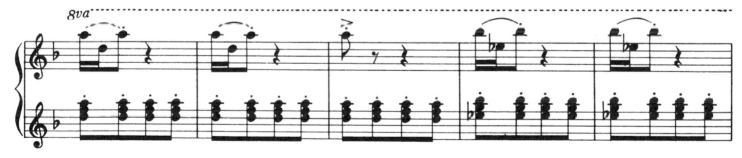

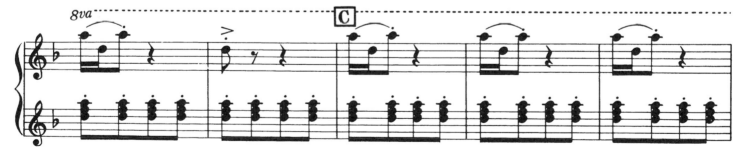

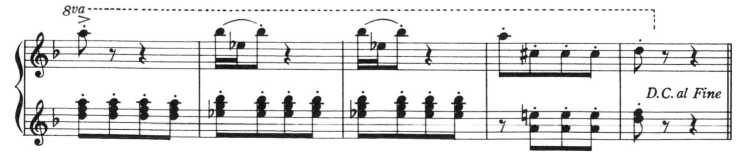

Little Rhapsody
on Hungarian themes

Denes Agay

Secondo

Little Rhapsody

on Hungarian themes

Primo

Denes Agay

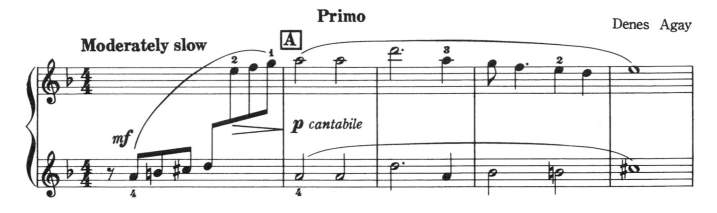

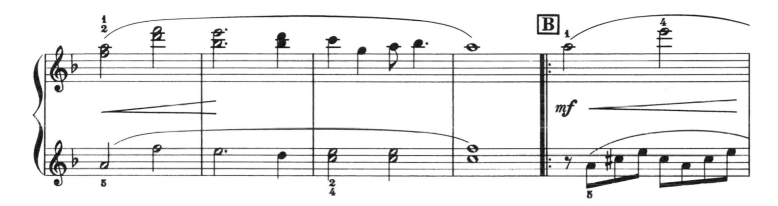

Secondo

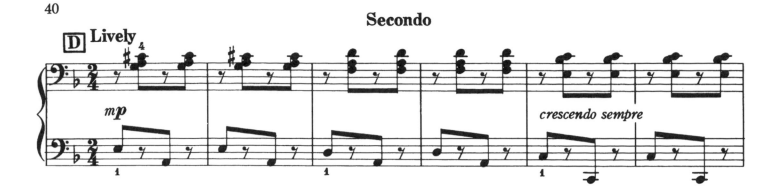

Primo

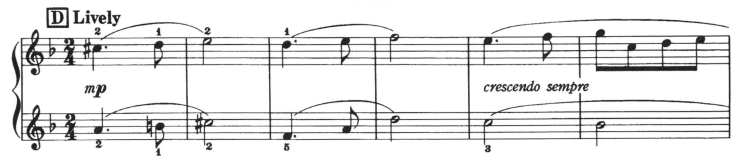

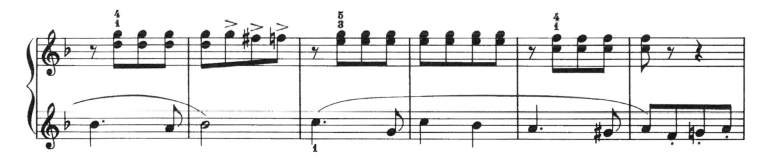
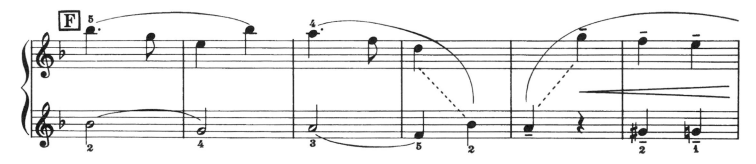

The "Merry Boys" Polka

Secondo

Franz von Suppé

Very bright

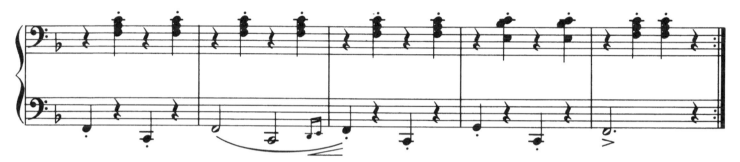

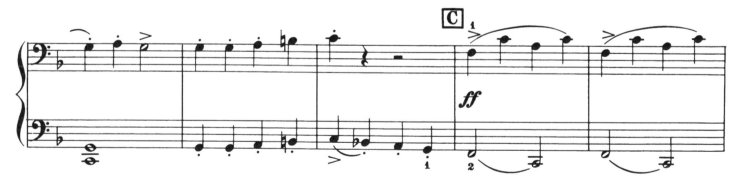

The "Merry Boys" Polka

Primo

Franz von Suppé

Very bright

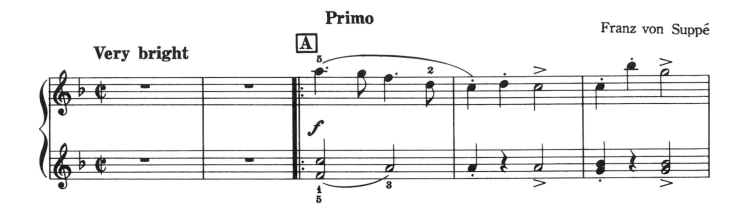

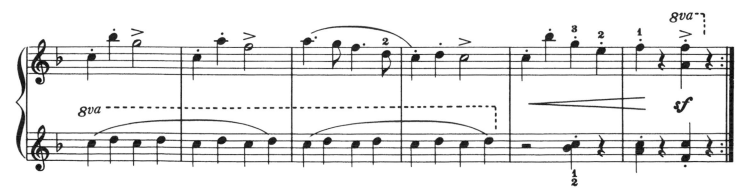

Waltzes
from "Fledermaus" and "Gypsy Baron"

Secondo

Johann Strauss

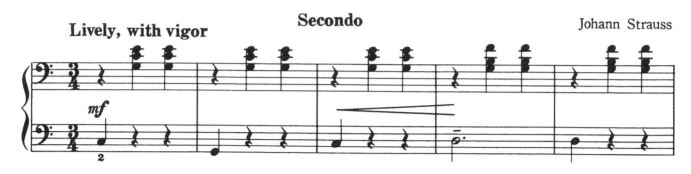

Waltzes
from " Fledermaus" and "Gypsy Baron"

Primo

Johann Strauss

Lively, with vigor

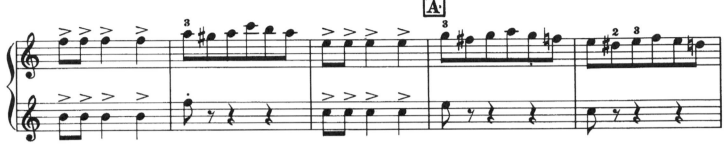

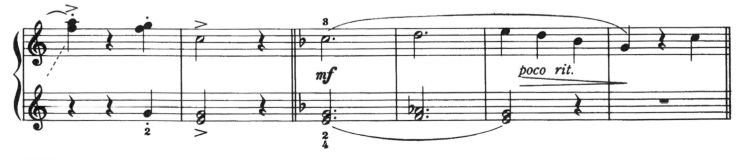

Secondo

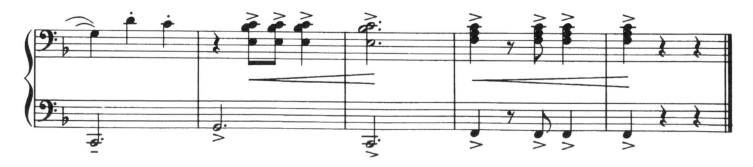

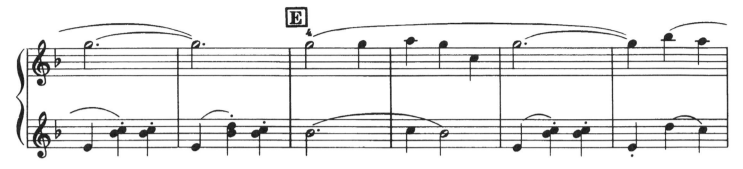

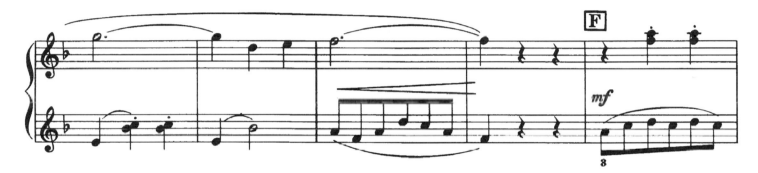

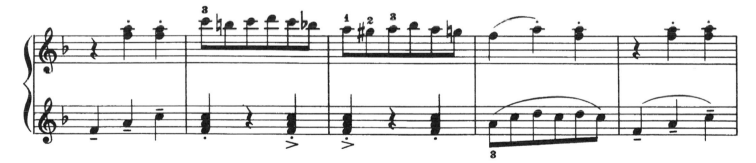

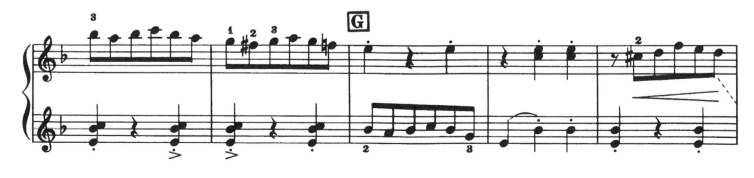

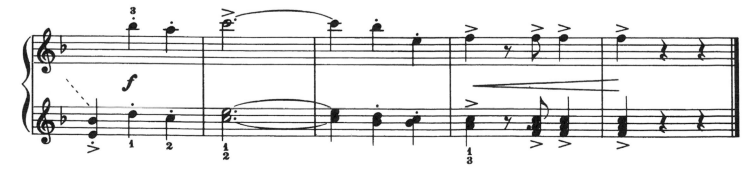

The Washington Post

Secondo

John Philip Sousa

Lively march tempo

The Washington Post

Primo

John Philip Sousa

Lively march tempo

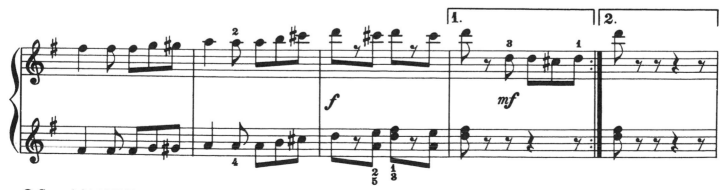

Secondo

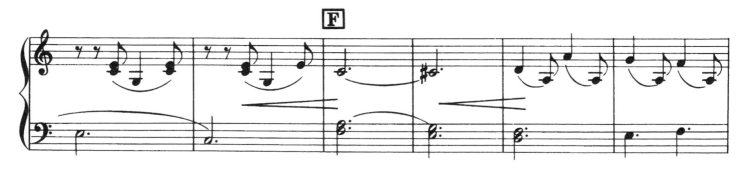

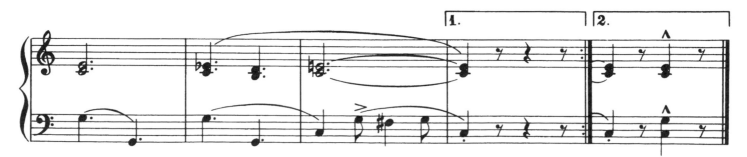

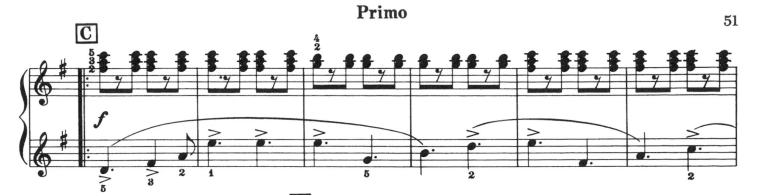

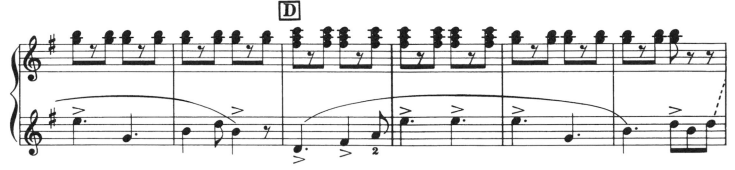

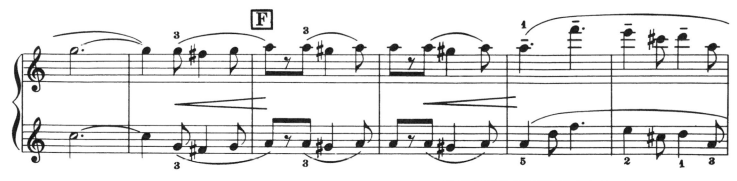

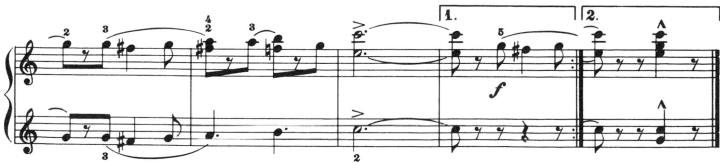

Fascination

Secondo

Filippo D. Marchetti

Fascination

Primo

Filippo D. Marchetti

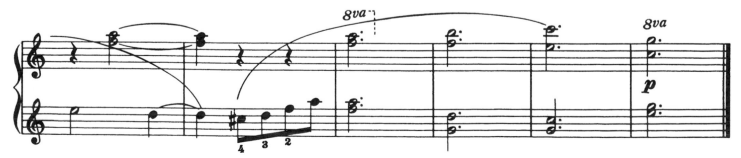

Can - Can
from the Operetta "La Vie Parisienne"

Jacques Offenbach

Secondo

Can-Can
from the Operetta "La Vie Parisienne"

Jacques Offenbach

Primo

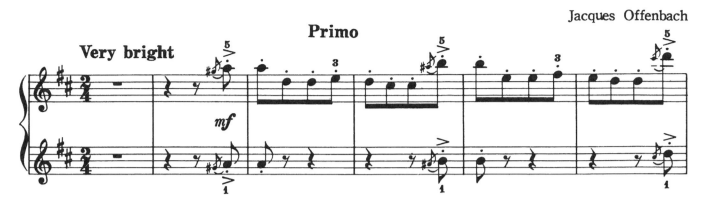

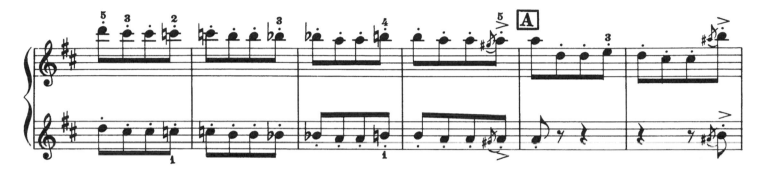

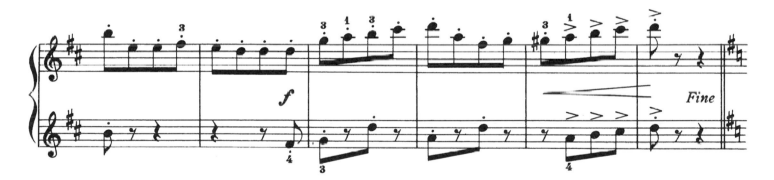

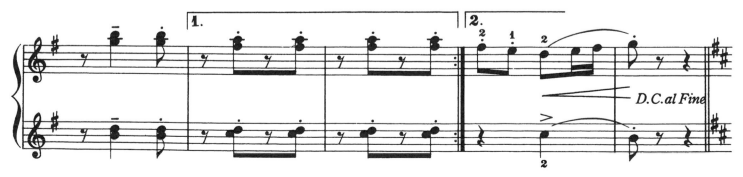

Parade Of The Tin Soldiers

Secondo

Leon Jessel

Graceful marching tempo

Parade Of The Tin Soldiers

Primo

Leon Jessel

Graceful marching tempo

Secondo

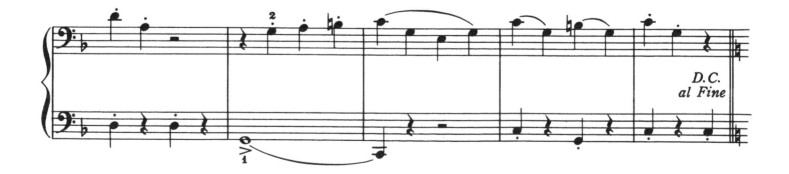

The Banjo Rag

Secondo

Charles Drumheller

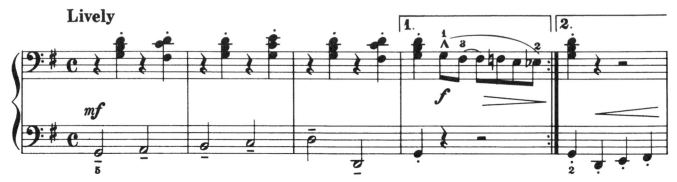

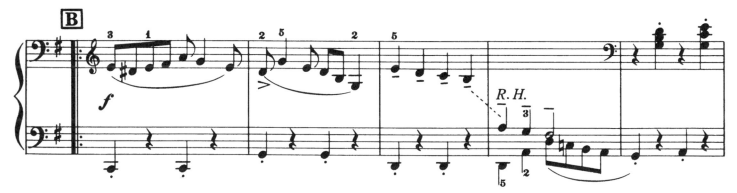

The Banjo Rag

Primo

Charles Drumheller

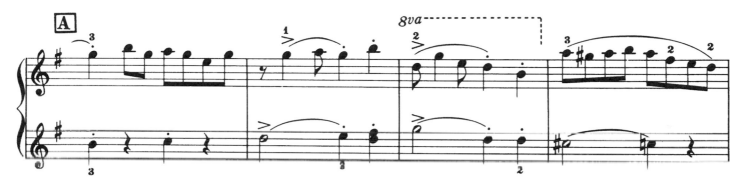
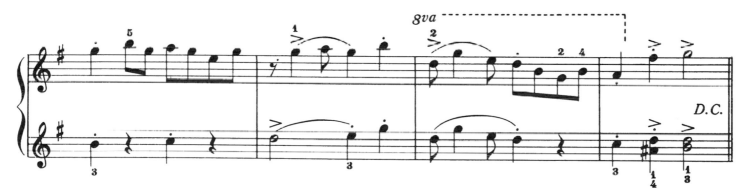

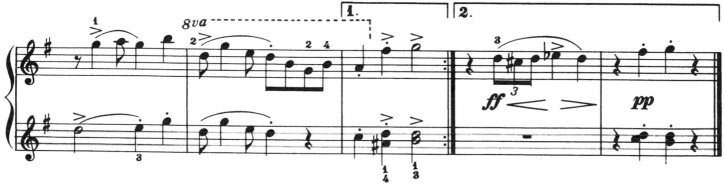

Careless Love

Secondo

Folk Song

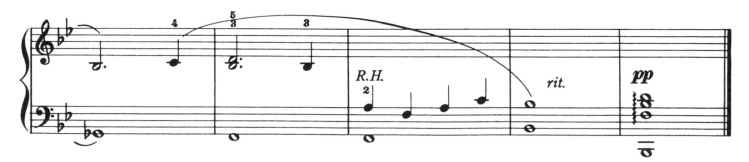

Careless Love

Primo

Folk Song

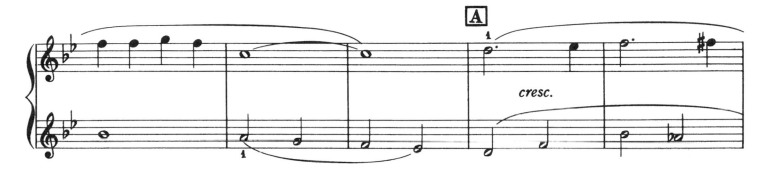

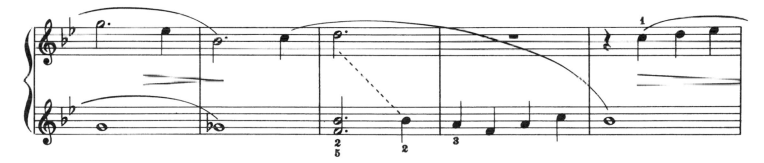

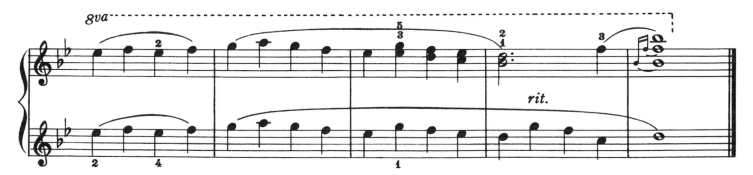

Arkansas Traveler

Secondo

Fiddle Tune

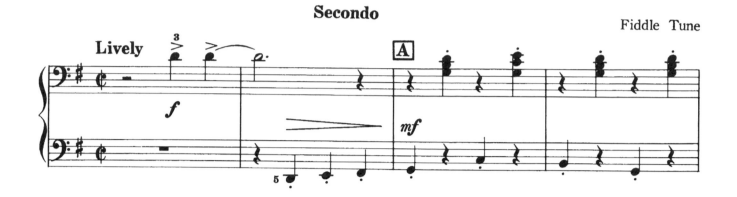

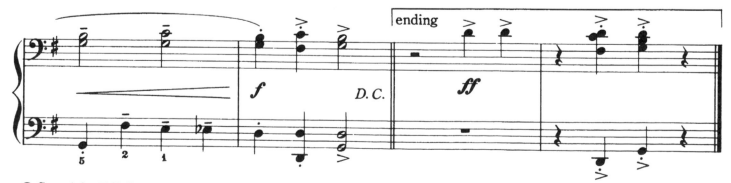

Arkansas Traveler

Primo

Fiddle Tune

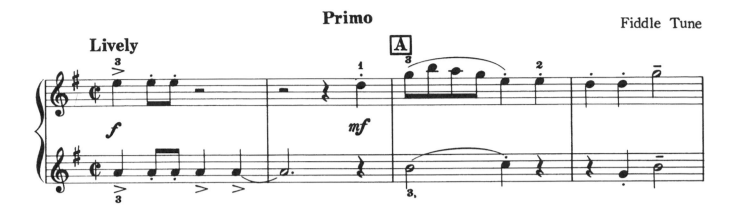

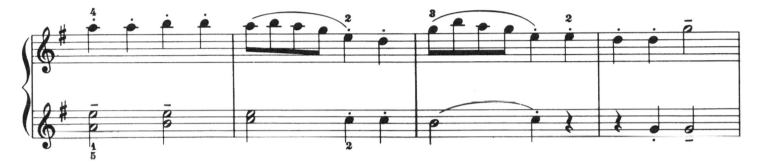

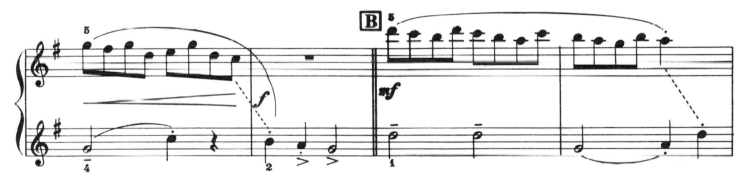

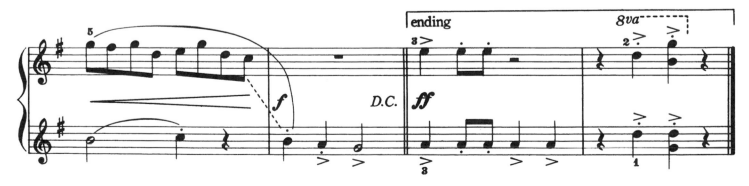

Hush-A-Bye
(All The Pretty Little Horses)

Secondo

Folk Lullaby

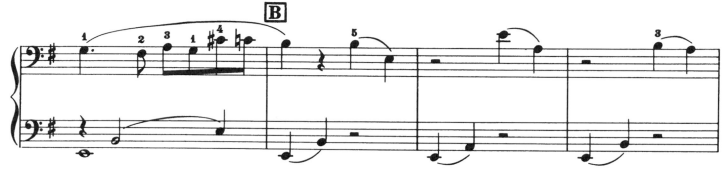

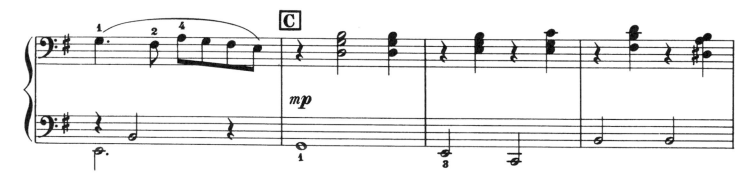

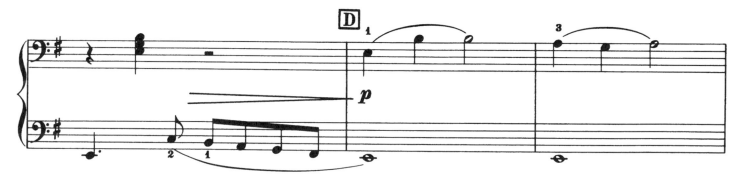

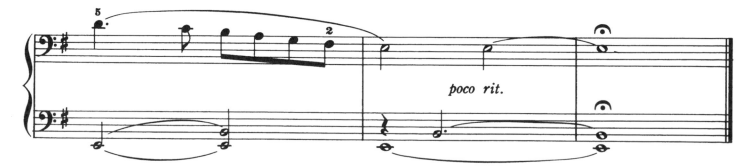

Hush-A-Bye
(All The Pretty Little Horses)

Primo

Folk Lullaby

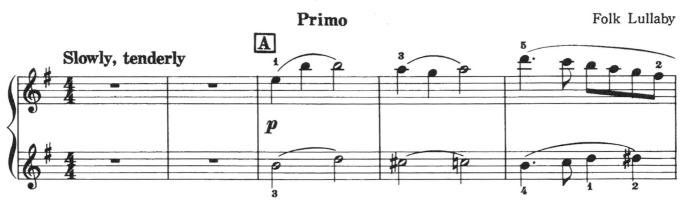

Adios Muchachos

Moderate tango tempo Secondo

Julio Sanders

Adios Muchachos

Moderate tango tempo   **Primo**   Julio Sanders

Boogie For Two

Secondo

Bright; with a rhythmic drive

Gerald Martin

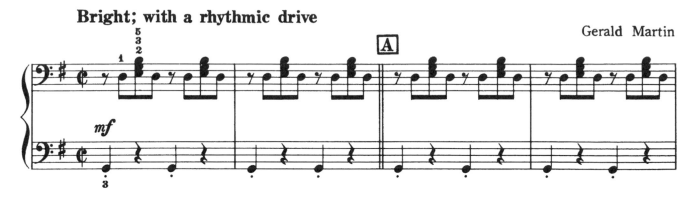

Boogie For Two

Primo

Gerald Martin

Bright; with a rhythmic drive [A]

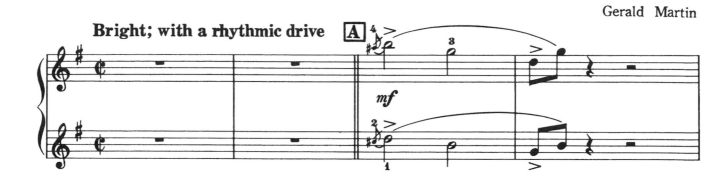

[B]

Secondo

Primo

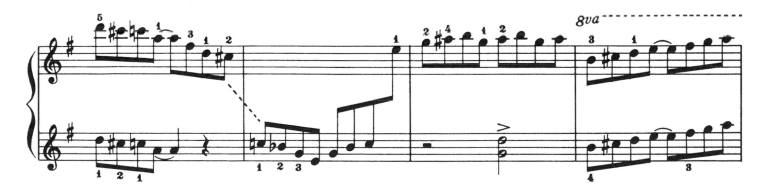

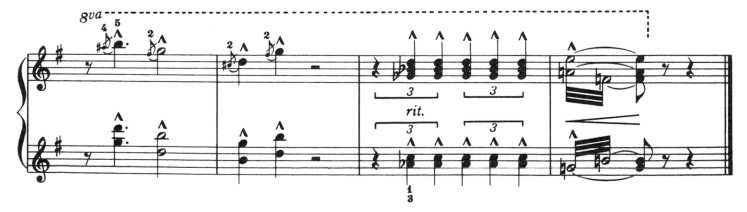

Give My Regards To Broadway

Secondo

George M. Cohan

Brightly

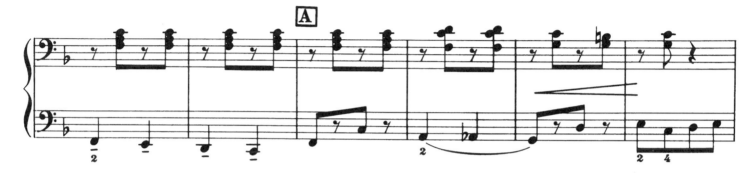

Give My Regards To Broadway

Primo

George M. Cohan

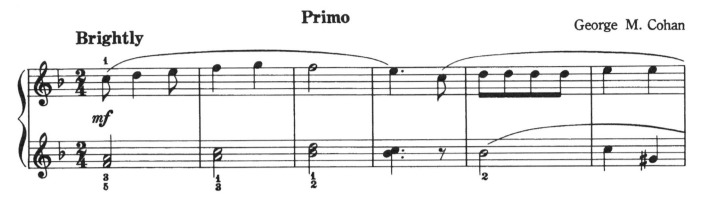

Jamaica Farewell

Secondo

Calypso Song

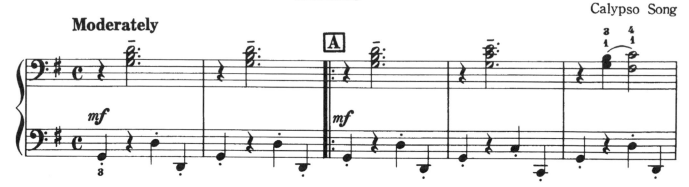

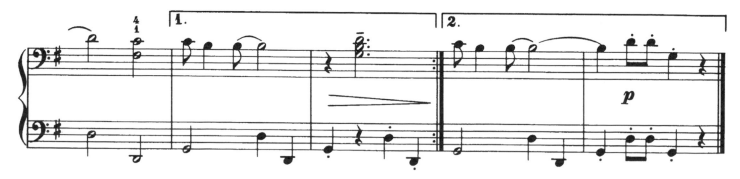

Jamaica Farewell

Primo

Calypso Song

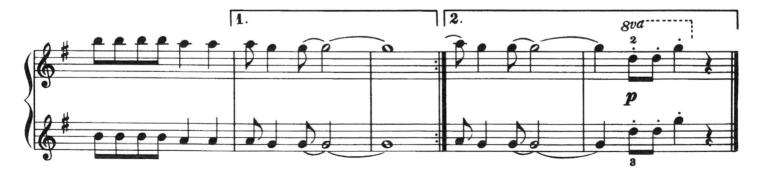

O Come All Ye Faithful

Adeste Fideles

Secondo

Old Latin Hymn

Spirited walking tempo

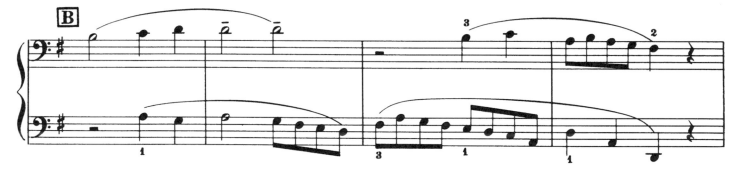

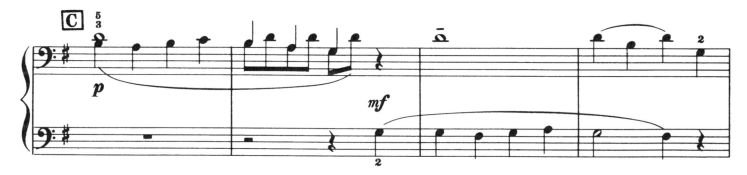

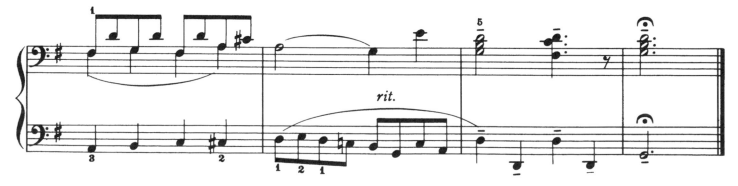

O Come All Ye Faithful

Adeste Fideles

Primo

Old Latin Hymn

Spirited walking tempo

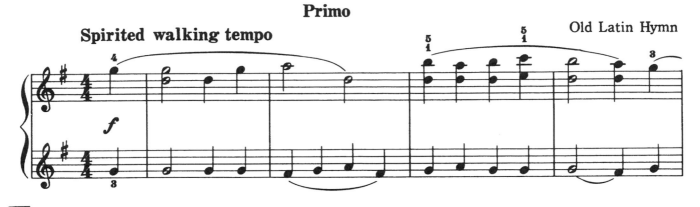

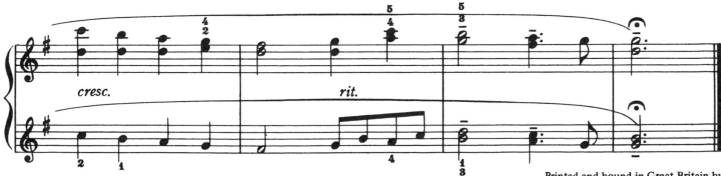

Printed and bound in Great Britain by
Caligraving Limited Thetford Norfolk